Book Eight - 1982.

THE MAGIC MOUSE AND THE MILLIONAIRE

HAMISH HAMILTON · LONDON

First published in Great Britain, 1982 by
Hamish Hamilton Children's Books
Garden House, 57-59 Long Acre, London WC2E 9JZ

British Library Cataloguing in Publication Data
McCrum, Robert
The magic mouse and the millionaire
I. Title II. Foreman, Michael
823'.914[J] PZ7
ISBN 0 241 10720 2

Colour Origination by
Adroit Photo Litho Ltd. Birmingham
Printed in Great Britain by
Balding and Mansell, Park Works, Wisbech

THE MAGIC MOUSE AND THE MILLIONAIRE

ROBERT McCRUM
ILLUSTRATED BY MICHAEL FOREMAN

The circus was in a terrible state. The liontamer and the clown were missing. Already the people were buying their tickets for the evening show. The ringmaster was furious.

"What can I do?" he said. "No clown, no laughter. No lion, no thrills. What can I do?" The corners of his silvery grey moustache began to droop. "They will all want their money back. We shall be ruined." Every day the circus gave two performances. One in the afternoon and one in the evening. After each performance the liontamer and the clown

were always very hot and cross. So, in the evening before the second show, they always had a drink together at the nearest public house.

The liontamer drank Guinness.

The clown usually had a whisky-and-soda.

Some days the clown would buy the drinks. On other days it would be the liontamer's turn. They were great friends. After their drink together they would walk back to the circus arm in arm. The liontamer was not hot. The clown was not cross. They were ready for the next show.

The clown and the liontamer loved the circus. A long time ago it had been the biggest and best circus in the land. In those days it had elephants and giraffes, apes and tigers, gazelles and bison, clowns, acrobats and jugglers, fire-eaters and The Strongest Man in the World.

Now it was very small. There was one old lion with a raggedy mane, and a couple of elderly horses. The clown always did his best to make people laugh, but times were hard. People didn't come to the circus any more. The circus had to travel to find the people. One week it was in Scotland. The next week it was in Wales. Sometimes it was in the big cities, and sometimes in the countryside. It was always on the move.

The liontamer and the clown were tired of all this travelling. One day they forgot whose turn it was to buy the drinks. (They were both a bit hard up.)

"Your turn I think," said the clown pleasantly.

"I beg your pardon," said the liontamer. "I bought the last round."

"You did not," replied the clown, with a snarl.

"I did," said the liontamer. And he gave the clown a punch on the nose.

"Ow!" said the clown, and he gave the liontamer a biff on the ear.

At this point a policeman arrived. "I'm going to arrest you," he said.

And he did. Very soon the liontamer and the clown were sitting behind bars. "We didn't even have a drink," said the clown sadly.

The local millionaire was driving home in his Rolls-Royce. He owned the town. He owned the factories, the shops and the football ground. He even owned the park where the circus was. The millionaire lived in a big house on the hill looking down on the town. He had a chauffeur, a butler, a housekeeper and a French cook. But he was lonely and rather unhappy.

Every day the millionaire took the early train to his office, as he had always done. Every day he made telephone calls to America and Japan. Every day he got a little bit richer. And at the end of the day, when everyone had gone home, his chauffeur came to collect him in the Rolls-Royce.

"Good evening sir," said the chauffeur.

"Good evening," said the millionaire, and opened the evening newspaper with a frown. But then he saw this huge advertisement.

CIRCUS! it said, in letters two inches high. The millionaire was sad. He remembered what the circus was like when he was a boy. He thought of the lights, the colours and the beautiful women. And when he remembered all the entertainment and the happy faces, he became excited.

"Hrrmmph!" he said, clearing his throat and trying to sound normal.

"Yes sir?" said the chauffeur, raising his bushy brown eyebrows.

"Drive past the park where the circus is," ordered the millionaire.

"Yes sir!" said the chauffeur, and put his foot on the accelerator. (The chauffeur loved animals.)

Inside the Big Top, the ringmaster was going bananas.

"Whatever shall I do?" he wailed. "No clown, no liontamer. We are all ruined."

The ringmaster's son was standing beside his father. "The show must go on," he said, even though he was only nine.

"This is no time for joking," snapped his father. "We can't use the lion without the liontamer. That lion is hungry. It will have the audience for dinner if we're not careful."

The ringmaster's son gave a little shiver. But he was nine and full of ideas. And when he thought hard his blue eyes sparkled.

"I've got an idea," he said, and he raced across the sawdust, out into the darkness.

Outside it was raining and the wind was cold. The ringmaster's son put his head down and sprinted. So he didn't see the smart-looking gentleman in the fur coat and the gold watch-chain coming towards him.

The millionaire's chauffeur was holding an umbrella over his master.

"I want a good seat in the front row," the millionaire was saying, "and . . . Ooooffff!!"

The ringmaster's son ran full tilt into the millionaire's fat grey waistcoat. "Ooops!" he puffed, out of breath.

"You should watch where you're going," said the millionaire crossly.

"Silly old fool," thought the ringmaster's son, and went on, running hard.

The ringmaster and his son lived in a strawberry-coloured caravan with sky-blue wheels. It had belonged to the ringmaster's gipsy grandfather and was full of treasures. Inside there was a Spanish banjo on a rusty nail, and a cuckoo clock that was always slow. There was a trick mirror that made the ringmaster's face go fat and thin when he trimmed his whiskers in the morning. The walls were covered with Persian rugs that the ringmaster said had belonged to a real emperor. On the back of the door was an old, old bell that jangled when the ringmaster's son burst in. In the middle of the caravan, hanging from a hook in the ceiling, was a dusty gilt birdcage. And there in the birdcage was a small white mouse.

The ringmaster's son loved his white mouse. His father had given it to him as a surprise when he was seven years old.

"This is a special mouse," he explained, "and it comes from far away."

So the boy took great care of the mouse. He fed it twice a day on milk and cheese, and he always took it to school for company. And when he wasn't busy in the Big Top he taught it tricks. The mouse could do anything. It could walk on its hind legs. It could dance in time to music. It could balance things on the end of its little pink nose. And sometimes it would vanish into thin air with a silent whisk of its long white tail. It was a magic mouse, of course.

"Come on, mouse," said the ringmaster's son, opening the cage. "This is your big break."

The millionaire had taken his seat. But as usual he was not happy. He thought his ticket was too expensive. His chair was hard and its back was broken. The Big Top was draughty and cold. Rain water was dripping through the canvas here and there. The audience was full of noisy children, and the millionaire, who didn't know much about children, liked them to be well-behaved.

"The circus wasn't like this in my day," he muttered under his breath.

Suddenly the lights went down. And there in the spotlight, in a scarlet and black coat trimmed with pure white silk, stood the ringmaster.

"Ladies and gentlemen," cried the ringmaster. "Good evening and welcome to the Big Top."

Everyone clapped.

"Tonight we are proud and delighted to present the finest circus in the world." Then he took out a parchment scroll with a flourish and read out the list of performers. He did not mention the clown and he did not mention the liontamer.

"Where are the clowns?" said a voice in the audience.

The ringmaster pretended he had not heard. He twirled his cloak and made a low bow. "Ladies and gentlemen, a big hand please for our opening number!"

Everyone clapped again. One or two people turned to each other and said: "But where are the clowns?"

The show was not a success. There were no lions and no clowns and the people were disappointed. The ringmaster was catching a cold and began to lose his voice. Even the millionaire's chauffeur, who was watching through a hole in the tent, said to himself, "It wasn't like this when I was a boy."

The millionaire became more and more unhappy. The frown on his face grew deeper and deeper. And his ears began to twitch as they always did when he was annoyed.

"This is a complete waste of money," he thought to himself. "Even the circus has gone to the dogs. Perhaps I shall have to go abroad after all."

But then the lights went down once more, and the ringmaster came in with a flourish and shouted (as well as he could):

"Maxim and the Magic Mouse!!!"

Standing in the spotlight was the ringmaster's son (who wasn't called Maxim at all, but he was nine and full of ideas). And there sitting on the brim of his black top hat was the magic mouse.

The people shuffled in their seats.

"I didn't come to watch white mice," snorted the millionaire.

But then the magic mouse began to perform and the audience watched in amazement.

The magic mouse danced in time to the music. It stood on its hind legs and did a somersault. It even vanished into thin air with a whisk of its long white tail. When the magic mouse reappeared again, the audience cheered, and the magic mouse squeaked, "Thank You."

Suddenly there was the sound of laughter.

"Sssshhhh!" said the audience.

But the laughter would not stop.

"SSSSSHHHHHHHHH!!!!!" said the ringmaster.

The millionaire was laughing.

The millionaire watched the magic mouse perform his magic tricks, and for the first time in his life he was happy. Once upon a time, when he was a boy, the millionaire had kept a white mouse. The magic mouse brought back happy memories. The millionaire laughed like a drain, a great gurgling laugh that started in the middle of his waistcoat and opened his mouth so wide that his head seemed about to split in half.

Then the audience laughed too and everyone was happy. The magic mouse came to the end of his act.

"More!" shouted the millionaire.

"MORE!!!" screamed the audience.

So the mouse did it all again. And the ringmaster forgot about the clown and the liontamer. His circus was a big hit after all!

After the show was over the millionaire walked round to the back of the Big Top. The ringmaster was congratulating his son, and the magic mouse was sitting on his shoulder nibbling a piece of Gruyère cheese. Everyone in the circus was excited.

"Come here, boy," said the millionaire, with a cunning smile. The rings on his fingers flashed in the moonlight.

The ringmaster's son looked at him cautiously. He recognised the smart-looking gentleman he had collided with before the show started.

"What do you want?" he asked. Under his breath he said, "You silly old fool."

"I want to buy the magic mouse," said the millionaire. "It makes me laugh."

"The magic mouse is mine," said the ringmaster's son. "And it's not for sale."

When the ringmaster overheard what the millionaire was saying to his son he pricked up his ears. He could do with some extra money. His feet were wet from the holes in his shoes and the Big Top needed mending.

"What will you pay for the magic mouse?" said the ringmaster to the millionaire.

"One hundred pounds," said the millionaire, taking out his wallet.

The ringmaster's son was upset. "The magic mouse is not for sale," he said.

"One thousand pounds," said the millionaire quickly.

The ringmaster looked at him. With that sort of money, he thought, I could buy a new lion.

"Ten thousand," he said.

"Done," said the millionaire, taking out his cheque-book.

So the millionaire took the magic mouse home to the big house on the hill. He put it on the back seat of his Rolls-Royce and sat in front with the chauffeur (who thought the magic mouse was a real star).

"I'm so excited," said the millionaire.

"Yes sir," said the chauffeur.

"A magic mouse!" said the millionaire.

"Yes sir," said the chauffeur, who felt sorry for the ringmaster's son.

"Oh, I'm so happy," said the millionaire.

"Yes sir," said the chauffeur, who felt sorry for the magic mouse as well.

Back at the circus, in the strawberry-coloured caravan, the ringmaster's son stared at the empty cage.

"I do hope the magic mouse is happier than I am," he said out loud. And two big tears rolled down his cheeks.

"Cuckoo," said the clock, late as usual.

The next day the millionaire woke up with a smile on his face.

"Isn't it a beautiful day?" he said to his butler at breakfast. "You must order lots of special cheeses," he told the French cook. "I have bought a magic mouse."

"Oo la la," said the French cook, who didn't understand a word of English.

"It does tricks," the millionaire explained to his housekeeper. "I'm so happy," he said.

And he gathered all his household into the dining room. He ordered fresh white linen to be laid. Then he took the magic mouse from its box and put it on the table. The French cook gave a little shriek of fright.

"It's all right," said the millionaire. "It will make you laugh."

The magic mouse sat on the table and looked at the butler, the French cook, the housekeeper and the millionaire.

"Off you go," said the millionaire. "Do your tricks. Vanish or something."

But nothing happened. The magic mouse sat there very still. Its sparkling eyes were dull. Its sharp white ears drooped and its white fur coat was ruffled and uncared for. It didn't even squeak.

"Go on," ordered the millionaire, "show us your tricks."

But the magic mouse did not move.

The butler, the housekeeper and the French cook all looked at each other and shook their heads sadly. Then very slowly they tiptoed out of the room.

The millionaire looked at the magic mouse for a long time. At last he said:

"You are sad, little mouse."

The magic mouse gave a small squeak.

"Yesterday," the millionaire went on, "I was sad and you were happy. You did amazing tricks and made me laugh. Now you look sad. Don't you like it here, magic mouse?"

The mouse twitched its whiskers as if to say, "No."

"Do you feel homesick?" he asked, stroking it gently with his fat forefinger.

And the magic mouse gave a sad little squeak as if to say, "Yes."

But when the millionaire sent his chauffeur out to bring the ringmaster and his strawberry-coloured caravan to live in the big house on the hill, he found that the circus had already moved on.

The millionaire didn't know what to do. He wanted his magic mouse to make him laugh.

"The magic mouse is homesick," he said to himself. "I must make it feel at home. Perhaps this place is too grand for a simple circus mouse. "That's it," he exclaimed out loud. "I must sell this house."

So the millionaire went to his banker and his lawyer on the top storey of a city skyscraper.

"I am selling my house," he said. "I am going to live in a circus caravan."

"Why?" they said.

"To make my magic mouse happy. Then it will do tricks. The magic mouse makes me laugh."

The banker and the lawyer looked at each other.

"Of course," they said, "we shall do whatever you say."

So the millionaire sold his house. He had to say goodbye to his butler, his housekeeper and his French cook as well. (They all thought the millionaire was going off his rocker and were not sorry to be going.)

Then the millionaire moved into a circus caravan. The first thing he found was that there was no room for his things. So he had to auction his pictures and his antique furniture. He had to sell off most of his fine clothes. Only the chauffeur, who liked animals (and who thought the magic mouse was a real star) wouldn't leave him. So the millionaire kept his Rolls-Royce.

"Now," said the millionaire to the magic mouse. "I have given everything away to make you feel at home. Now you must be happy. So, please, will you do your tricks and make me laugh?"

But the magic mouse did not move.

The next day the millionaire set off on the early train to work as usual.

"Well," he thought. "I can always find happiness in my work. I can always make money."

But it was no good. He couldn't concentrate. He telephoned Japan, but all the time he was thinking of the magic mouse. For the first time in his life he made a mistake and lost half his fortune.

"Never mind," he said. "This afternoon I'll telephone America." But when he got through to New York he was still thinking of the magic mouse and he made another big mistake. This time he lost the other half of his fortune.

So he went home to his caravan on the hill a poor man, and he took the magic mouse into the palm of his hand.

"You've ruined me, little mouse," said the millionaire. "Please make me laugh again. Then it will have been all worthwhile."

The magic mouse squeaked a sad squeak as if to say, "I'm sorry, but I'm sad too."

The chauffeur, who was preparing to say goodbye, overheard what his master was saying.

"Excuse me sir," said the chauffeur, "but that mouse misses the ringmaster's son. We must find the circus again, if you don't mind my saying so, sir."

At once the magic mouse sat up and began to jump up and down with excitement. He did a back flip somersault, just to show them. His little brown eyes were sparkling.

"Start the Rolls," ordered the millionaire. "We're going to find that circus."

"Yes Sir!!!" said the chauffeur, and saluted.

The circus had moved on down the road. It was performing by the seaside. The liontamer and the clown had been set free. The ringmaster had spent the millionaire's ten thousand pounds very well. He had bought elephants and dancing zebras. He had bought a new lion with a terrific roar. He had repaired the Big Top. He was even able to hire The Strongest Man in the World again.

The summer holiday-makers filled the circus night after night.

The new lion roared.

The audience went OOOOOHHHH!!!!!

The circus was making money and everyone was happy – everyone except the ringmaster's son. He did not laugh and he did not smile. When he was alone his eyes were full of tears. He was pining for his magic mouse.

One evening the ringmaster's son was sitting sadly outside the strawberry-coloured caravan with the sky-blue wheels, watching the sun set below the horizon. Into the fairground drove a Rolls-Royce.

"I know that car," said the ringmaster's son, jumping up with excitement. "It's the millionaire's!" And the ringmaster's son flew over to the car park.

When the magic mouse saw the ringmaster's son, it went crazy with happiness. It danced and it pranced, and it did a somersault. It balanced things on the end of its little pink nose. How the millionaire laughed!

The ringmaster was on his way to prepare for the evening show when he heard the strange noise.

"I've heard that laugh somewhere before," he said out loud.

And round the corner of the tent he found his son and the magic mouse doing tricks for the millionaire, who was laughing his head off.

"I've given away all my things and lost all my money," he said, "so that this magic mouse would make me happy, and I never realised! All I had to do was find the circus! How happy I am at last! Please will you let me join," he begged. "It won't cost anything and I'm quite good with money you know."

"Of course," said the ringmaster, twirling his silvery moustache. And he gave his son a special wink, as if to say, "I knew it would be all right in the end."

The magic mouse soon became the talk of the town. Everyone wanted to see it. The circus was an even bigger success. The ringmaster ordered new costumes for everyone. The chauffeur was taught how to drive an elephant and got a place in the Grand Finale.

"I've always wanted to be in the circus," he said.

The millionaire looked after the money they made. Twice a day he watched the mouse do tricks. Twice a day he laughed till he cried. And once a day he took the money to the bank.

"Good afternoon sir," said the bank manager. "You're looking very well sir." The bank manager couldn't help noticing that the millionaire was wearing jeans. "Are you on holiday sir?"

"Don't call me sir," said the millionaire with a smile. "I've joined the circus. Every day is a holiday."

The millionaire was as happy as he could remember.

The ringmaster's son (who was nine and full of ideas) asked his father: "Where did you get that mouse?"

But the ringmaster never told.